POSTURES, PRAYERS, AND POEMS

POSTURES, PRAYERS, AND POEMS

A Yoga Journey Through Earth, Body, and Soul

JOSEPH LAURICELLA

gatekeeper press

Columbus, Ohio

Postures, Prayers, and Poems:
A Yoga Journey Through Earth, Body, and Soul

Published by Gatekeeper Press
2167 Stringtown Rd, Suite 109
Columbus, OH 43123-2989
www.GatekeeperPress.com

ISBN (paperback): 9781642375664

Printed in the United States of America

ACKNOWLEDGEMENTS

I wish to thank my parents, who continue to teach me the healing power of love and devotion. I want to acknowledge the thousands of people and students who have participated in my classes, retreats, and trainings over the years. You're the reason this book came to life, from my heart to yours, thank you. Most likely, none of us would be practicing yoga if it weren't for Sri Tirumalai Krishnamacharya who went to the top of the world for many years to learn and eventually share this ancient wisdom. Heartfelt gratitude for you, TKV Desikachar, and all the others who have devoted their lives to teaching the heart of yoga in the Great Tradition. I bow to you all. A special thanks to Stacy Levy for her love, support, encouragement, and feedback through the many stages and development of this book. Elyce Neuhauser for her eagle eyes of editing, loving support, and enthusiastic push to bring this book into the world. Sara Connell continues to coach me, guide me, and lift me with her bright light and courageous energy. To Reverend Gregory Wiest for his friendship, our wordsmith wrestling matches, spiritual direction, and always holding positive space. Kiya Shaun for always believing in me and being a source of light in my life. Chris Melco for his spiritual guidance, friendship, ceremony, and no bullshit way of being. Michael Smith for being my first real yoga teacher who instilled the importance of technical breath work and yoga training in the early days. Baron Baptiste for his bold, powerful, and unapologetic teacher trainings that helped me hone my skills as a teacher and leader.

To all of my teachers of yoga, of Lakota spirituality, of ceremony here now and on the other side: Michael Hopp, Wallace Black Elk, Servando, Scott Thomas, I bow to you.

With great reverence, I acknowledge the wisdom keepers across all cultures. The men and women of the past and present who have protected and shared the sacred ways, often at great risk to their own well-being. I thank the devoted ones who've walked in the ceremonial ways of prayer and healing for all the creatures living on the earth. To my late wolfdog Codi, the messenger, and to my divine dog Shiva, an incarnate of a high priestess. To all those who have so powerfully and compassionately helped to bring this book into the world, I thank you.

CONTENTS

INTRODUCTION

*Inhale, and God approaches you. Hold the
inhalation and God remains with you.
Exhale, and you approach God. Hold the
exhalation and surrender to God.*

Sri Tirumalai Krishnamacharya

In 1997, I adopted a wolf-dog. Overwhelmed with his care, I drove him cross country to a wolf refuge in the Colorado Rockies. I loved him so much that I couldn't leave him there, so I stayed. I worked and lived among forty wolves without electricity or running water or even a bathroom. My yoga practice began on a small deck just outside the door of a tiny cabin. The platform hovered a few feet above a trickling brook where howls echoed through the canyon. I've been practicing and teaching yoga ever since.

I enjoyed living off grid and close to the earth. So close that I became just another tree in the forest as I reached up rooted, another wolf with four paws on the ground digging in, and a neighbor to a red tailed hawk I named George, who visited me in the afternoons. On weekend evenings a small gathering of us sang Lakota prayer songs in a sweat lodge with a Native American elder. Soon my postures and body movements became prayers and my prayers became poems that found their way through the oxygen rich mountain air that enveloped my body and soul.

While I built a relationship with the wolves and the landscape. A subtle, yet powerful truth permeated through, that we are all part of the land no matter where we live. We are in fact not separate from the earth itself. All indigenous cultures know this and have been speaking this truth since the first European settlers arrived in America. In fact, most tribes thought to secure a way of life for seven generations into the future. Co-existing is not optional, it is essential to our survival. This became my mantra, and my mission is to reconnect people to this understanding: we are an integral part of the earth, yoga connects us to source, what we do to her, we do to ourselves. We are in fact not separate. The more people who experience this within their being, the healthier we become together. As a species, we must collectively reconnect to the truth or continue to suffer the consequences of climate change and mass extinction of animals, including us. Yoga is the first step in caring for the planet. Why? It's how we all got here.

Yoga is the union of opposites, which took place when your parents' two cells became one and you were conceived. Inside your mother's womb you received a beating heart, brain, and spine. The probability of you being born is one in 400 trillion. A scientific miracle. Think about that. You have a better chance of winning the lottery, yet here you are. You are not an accident no matter what your circumstance is today or who your parents are. You are a living miracle! The question then becomes: how will you shape your miracle?

The very first thing you did when you emerged from your mother was take a profoundly deep inhalation. The outside air entered your lungs and your life began. The world shaped and molded you like clay and you became the person you are today. The very last thing you'll ever do in this life is exhale. Yoga is a celebration and participation in life through the inhale and exhale (Sadhana). When we direct our attention and unite the breath cycles (pranayama) while moving through postures (Asana) in a logical sequence (Vinyasa Krama), meditation (Dharana) occurs naturally. Along with a calm space after practice comes self-acceptance, love, compassion, strength, tolerance, and peace to name a few. Please understand, yoga is not about attaining or getting good at yoga postures. It's simply an intimate connection with the function of life in a gradual progression of postures (Vinyasa). Contained in these postures lives our life's story. Yoga practice helps us empty out and awaken to our true reality, our true nature whatever that may be.

Sri T. Krishnamacharya, the father of contemporary yoga and the teacher of all teachers taught that: yoga practice must incorporate conscious breathing and be adapted to the individual based on age, body type, health condition, and cultural background. This interplay immediately unites us with source. Source gives us life in the form of an electric current that beats our heart as well as the earth that provides our food, water, and air.

I practiced yoga with the wolves on that deck in the heart of the Rocky Mountains over twenty years ago, yet I remember every moment that I felt at one with, and at peace with, everything. This is the spiritual aspect of yoga that many seek and it is literal and ordinary. You don't need to be in a forest or a church. You don't need to contort your body into a sophisticated posture. You don't have to search for something outside of yourself. Your body is the temple. Your breath is the bridge. Your mind is the conductor. Woven together, you receive instant access to your own life energy. You can move past your identity, past your inner critic to land in a state of pure consciousness. There's nothing more spiritual than this understanding. In fact, the word "spirit," is derived from "spiritus," which is the Latin term for breath. When you're with your breath, you're with spirit.

Do your daily Yoga practice: postures with breathwork and sitting still in a seamless transition that is practical, accessible, and intelligent. Breathing in direct intimacy with body movement is not just healthy, it raises your consciousness and therefore evolves humankind. It's like taking medicine. It is literally your birth right, an interaction with source no matter what faith or religion you follow and no matter what culture you live in. Yoga strengthens your constitution, soothes your soul, and shapes your miracle of life.

We have an extraordinary potential to unite humans across continents. Yoga is the missing link that connects the most intelligent species to the rest of the kingdom. It's time to plug into source and respond to our reality. Simply put, if you want to do something good for yourself and the planet, practice some yoga every day.

Wolves howl to communicate, congregate, and contribute to a greater whole. Humans do yoga. This book is a call to action. I hope that you not only let the words move something inside you, but that you act on what most resonates with your passion and purpose to contribute to the greater good. I hope that you use the journal in the back of the book for your gratitude list, your thoughts, feelings, visions and goals. If you already have your own yoga practice, perhaps it's time to teach others. You can begin a yoga practice at any age, for it changes as we change, grows as we grow, slows as we slow.

The poems and prayers in the pages ahead share my inner world of yoga through my experience of over 20 years of practicing and teaching. They're from both the teacher and student of yoga and the wisdom keepers of the indigenous peoples. They go beyond the posture, or at least past the physical form in an attempt to honor the internal process of life and our relationship with the earth that still supports us every day. These postures, prayers, and poems are themselves an offering. Take your time with them. Sit with them. I hope they serve you, inspire you, or even entertain you in the best of ways, perhaps stir that which rests inside you untapped, yet ready to emerge into the light.

Enter through the breath. Guruji said.
Enter what? The student asked.
Yes. The teacher replied.
I enter what?
Exactly. Said the master.

YOU ARE YOGA

It's all Yoga.
You don't need to find yoga. You don't even need
to strike a pose.
You are yoga.
It's not in a class or a studio or a gym.
Yoga is not out there as if separated from your
very existence.
It's in you as you right now.
You don't have to go anywhere, not to India or
an ashram.
Practice yoga in your kitchen or living room or
backyard.
Connect to life support system in seconds.
Create the space for a satisfying inhalation, feel
the air flow all the way in,
and all the way back out, this is yoga.
A four count with your breath even, deserving of
your attention.

Take another breath in as you reach your arms above your head,
pause at the top, spread your fingers to feel the sky,
exhale your arms and hands all the way down,
pause, the earth supports you from below.
Repeat.
Work to synchronize meticulously.
Two separate things become one.
Breath action and movement merge into mind-fulness.
Many parts, one yoga.
One thing, this is yoga.
This one thing is everything.
Take another breath and move with it.
You can find a teacher to help.
You are the yoga.
Don't worry about doing it the perfect way.
You are the way.
Breathe more, feel more. Healing is on the way.

SUN SALUTATION
(SURYA NAMASKAR)

In ancient times the sun was everything.

No sun no life.

Inside your mother's womb your whole body was coiled around your heart.

It was dark, but a light from the spark of the beat of the heart was your source.

Your birth exposed you to a new light.

The sun is your birthright, source, fuel, food.

In ancient times we looked to the east waiting for the sun to rise.

As it came up, we reached up.

As it rose, we rose.

We stepped back, we opened up.

Moved like the sun in a circle.

We went down on the ground, then stood up again
like a baby learns to walk.

The sun every day, many days to the moonlight.

The western sky brings on the night.

In the darkness of the early morning we pray for the
sun to shine again and again and again.

CHILDS POSE
(BALASANA)

Hello sweet child, coiled, wild.

Take care of the self.

Return to the fetal place when life doesn't feel safe.

Back to where you started, surrendered space.

Protect your perception,
discern what the world shares.

Reveal daily doses of peace and send
it out from this nurturing place.

Accept it like a prayer, give it to the people,
and live grateful today.

Grateful as a grandfather, humble on his knees,
thinking like a child running through tall weeds
and grass-stained years of adolescent dreams.

STANDING AT ATTENTION (SAMASTHITI)

Red Running Bear, a medicine man, spoke to a group of kids and their parents.

He said, "all things want to be understood, a bird, an elk, a tree, a rock, a human. Once we agree with this understanding, respect naturally follows."

We all want to be seen for who we are. The unveiling of the true self is to appreciate simply standing in your body, in your God-given right.

Speak your truth, take your place in this life on this earth, plant your feet, look forward, stand confidently, attentively, unapologetically.

MOUNTAIN POSE
(TADASANA)

Travel through all the bones to the feet,
root down into the dirt, the earth.
Stand like a rock with roots.
Reach up to a new day
wake up
rise up
get up
look up
offer it up
lift thy spirit high.
Reach for the sun
like a plant
toward the light.
Hands open from the I,
grows into father sky.
God enters through inhales.
Exits through exhales
You are the vessel bridging the air of the sky
with the earth that cries for understanding.
Like a mountain
to the sea

she cries in me.
Your truth is the body.
Land in it.
The land is the body.
Dwell in it.
You are a steward to this place.
Respect it, protect it like your child.
Stand taller in the face of the takers.
Give breath back to the mountains.
Do this for the people
for the children
for the generations of earth dwellers.

STANDING FORWARD BEND (UTTANASANA)

Every time I bend forward and down in the direction below, I bow to the old ways, the wise ones, the elders, those worthy to look up to, who passed along knowledge to children who listened for hours.

I surrender to gravity and release my spine to the divine, grab my feet and pull down.

A power bow to mother earth, to everyone who has taken care of me, touched my life abundantly.
I bow down to the ones who serve the people, who hold the light of hope for innocent children of emotional prisons.

Hinging from the center, a cold winter or worn out leather, tie the boots or go without shoes, walk with your heart full and feet light as a feather.

HALF WAY LIFT
(ARDHA UTTANASANA)

I learn to hold my torso parallel to the floor, look down, listen to the sounds.

I'm not all the way up or all the way down, but my legs stand strong.

Two worlds collide along my spine, the one below where the four-legged roam,

the one above where birds fly.

Listen to the animals Gandhi said, morality lives in how we treat them.

I open my heart toward the listening, eyes focused, breathing.

I hear ten thousand buffalo souls pounding the ground, tears well up and drop down.

LOW PLANK
(CHATURANGA DANDASANA)

As I hover above the earth's surface, my childhood passes through my hands.

I have grappled, questioned my direction, stumbled on life's tragedies, learned from books, and asked on my knees for purpose.

Engage the core, contract the legs.

My heart pounds hovering above the ground, senses sound.

I push and pull at the same time, feet flexed, time still.

Something rises up from below, permeates my hands, then my limbs.

I hear footsteps on the grass like a train on the tracks, tremors ride along my spine and a voice echoes over me, *let go of the past.*

UPWARD FACING DOG
(URDVHA MUKHA SVANASANA)

Lie on the ground belly-side down.
Plant your hands as if they are feet inside sneak-
ers gripping the street.
Pull your upper body forward.
Lift your sternum.
Drag the lower half, infuse your legs, bare your
chest.
The soul is in there, placed before birth.
Look inside your heart as your tissues pull apart
like curtains open on stage.
The mind plays tricks, but your body never lies.
It tells the truth like a stream cuts through
granite in time.
Shhhh. Listen.

DOWNWARD FACING DOG
(ADHO MUKHA SVANASANA)

A wolf perspective.

Hands become feet bare to the touch.

A life fueled by love not more stuff.

Tied from my heels to my sits, rawhide strips drying.

A neutral spine suspended in time, a pyramid in the forest.

I claw the ground; my front claws dig in for truth.

Clean dirt, trees, and deep roots.

Please stop fracking, my paws hurt.

As my head hangs down, I hear whispers, go back to the earth.

Bring the people down, take a look around like children do.

Listen to the wisdom glisten, morning dew.

FIERCE POSTURE
(UTKATASANA)

Lightning strikes every second minute hour day
in and day out.
A tiny spark beats your heart.
Electric we are.
Our nerves, wires conducting currents.
Allow us to feel and move.
Opposites balance.
Hips lower, heart higher.
Legs bend, arms straighten, spine lengthens.
Breathe in, breathe out.
The body a vessel.
A vehicle of emotion in motion, yoga.
Transition, liberation, moksha.

MOTHER EARTH
(PRITHVI MATA)

Remember mother when you do your yoga.

When you roll out your piece of earth like a red carpet.

The mat is not made of dirt, but it represents her support.

Mother, she is life.

What we do to her, we do to ourselves.

She takes shape by how we treat her, and the people.

Acknowledge her as you age and move upon her.

When you finally rest she will be there to catch you.

The wind will tell your story through chimes, the way it does.

Remember to give back to her when you do your yoga.

A breath, a bow, an open-handed prayer, a chant to share.

Her rainforests, air, and medicine. Her oceans nutrition. Her landscape is like our skin. Her dirt our flesh. Her rock our bone. Her streams our veins. Her water our blood. Her trees our hair. Her emotion our history. Her thoughts our decisions. Her health our life.

Please remember mother when you do your yoga.

YOGA TEACHER

A teacher, not an instructor.
Transmitter, not a judger.
Deliberate thinker, problem dissolver.

One who acknowledges the unseen.
Knows how to give the view,
in dosages, rather than skews.

Not a threat, but a soldier.
Trains the shadow to open
what the self cannot see.
Drags potential to the edge,
summons the courage to step off.

Hurricanes break egos,
follow the center.
Asana one tool,
stillness the holy other.

Inhale sunlight waters flow.
Purification of all relations.
A crocheted blanket, new fallen snow.

SHADOW SPIRIT

Oh, Shadow Spirit
When you question every move
My heart aches

The authority
Of my will to defend honor
Breaks

You win
I'm not worth
The energy it takes

It's easier
To medicate
Than face my mistakes

I shine beneath the surface
like silver
Tarnished

You want me to look good
Live a lie
Fake lonely smiles

I know so well
Failure fuels
When love lights the way

Yet
I sit in the corner
Wrapped in a blanket

Face the window
Waiting
For a single ray of sun

GREAT SPIRIT
(WAKAN TANKA)

There's something watching me, moving
inside me, loving me. I feel you.
When I look into the eyes of a
baby, or a sunrise, I see you.
When I hear birds chirping and the
wind blowing, I know you.
When I chew a blackberry plucked
from the vine, I taste you.
My search for you has led me back
to where it all began, right here.

Oh, Great Spirit help me to get myself
out of the way, so your creative force
moves through me with direction, guides
me with purpose. I will listen.

Keep me lifted above my own brutal war, so that I can help repair the sacred web that weaves through all things.

Give me the strength to accept the responsibility of service, to awaken the sleepers and stay awake for the teachers. Steer me into action that most honors the sacredness of life and the sanctity of death. Let me stay humble, so humble, but give me the words and actions to reach the hearts of the people, beyond their insecurities to connect them to the source of all life.

SWEAT LODGE
(INIPI)

We crawl inside a narrow opening one after another.
Sit down on the dirt next to the person we followed.
A circle forms the way a plant grows.
Ancient stones placed in the center glow.
The canvas flap closes after the last person enters.
The blackness swaddles me.
A drum beat begins.
BOOM, boom.
BOOM, boom.
The medicine man pours water on the stones.
BOOM, boom.
They hiss.
BOOM, boom.
The breath of mother whispers.
BOOM, boom.
Singing begins.
Wakan Tanka.
The beat grows louder.
BOOM, boom.

BOOM, boom.
My flesh softens.
Bones dig in.
Thoughts vanish.
Mother sighs.
BOOM, boom.
I start to cry.
BOOM, boom.
And cry.
BOOM, boom.
Try to offer prayers.
Stuck words stumble out of my mouth.
Thank....
Voices merge in the air above.
A new song, faster beat.
boom boom boom boom boom.
Drum beats echo around.

Hot rain streams down.

BOOM, boom. BOOM, boom. BOOM, boom.

BOOM.

The flap opens.   We crawl out.   Stars dark.

MINDFULNESS

Talking with breath, the breath to talk.
Walking with breath, the breath to walk.
Living with breath, the breath to live.
Watch it for some time, become the witness.
The witness is no seeker, the
witness is your teacher.
Now.
Now.
Now.

CRESCENT LUNGE
(ANJANEYASANA)

We seek the truth, satyam.

We wander through time, I am.

Raise our wands to the aliens swirling around like flies.

Have we been here before?

An ancient painting hangs on the wall with a light in the sky so bright,

but it's during the day not a star in the night.

Calling out to the God of light.

Oh, radiant light waiting inside, may your rays pierce through my flesh and shine out from the depths of my heart.

MEDITATION

The conscious breath reveals what
the moving mind conceals.
If you want to see the truth,
stop, sit, and breathe.
Just sit still and breathe, your movie will start.
The first time you sit still, eyes closed,
might rattle you to the core.
You might even abandon your seat when your
thoughts collide like strangers on a street.
Unfamiliar, but not strangers.
Sit again and again.
Let the voices speak without reacting.
There's no danger sitting someplace
safe to claim your inner space.
The truth, satyam, is the master
key to heal old wounds.
The hurts and regrets are buried
in the dirt of your flesh.

Time doesn't heal all by itself,
sometimes it just covers things up.
Healing occurs through what we rediscover.
To make things right expose
the story to the light.
If you sit with your thoughts long enough,
you may realize that you are not them,
and they're not yours, like feathers.
Ride the feelings all the way to the source.
Make amends, write the letter, say I'm
sorry, forgive the self or another.
Choose healing even if you're dying,
treat the person not the problem.
Birds shed old feathers.

TWISTING CRESCENT LUNGE
(PARVRITTA ANJANEYASANA)

Ladders have rungs like vertebrae.
Molecular structure, channels, DNA.
Vertebrae are wider at the base.
Take the weight of gravity.
Flashes braid their way around
powerlines without boundaries,
taper with another ring.
Wires wrapped and woven merge
membranes liquid not frozen, sap runs.
The frontal fascia lines grow long,
wrung out cold wash cloths
soothe summer sun burn,
while Ferris wheels turn, cotton candy
spun, and stuffed animals watch from
rooftops of little trailers selling fun.

SUNSET

Worship the sun; the sun is no judge.
She shines on my face with no rules.
I worship the sun, but don't pray to the sun like
a God.
I don't ask it for anything more.
What more could I possibly ask for?
Leaves on greens are edible, horses, deer, rabbits.
Pumpkins turn orange in the cold mornings.
No need to pray for more stuff,
I pray with prose in rows and yoga poses.
As she goes down to bring on the night
I stare directly into her rays of light

THE TEACHING

I'm the teacher, but I need the teaching.
The words are not mine.
They come from some other place,
but I believe them.
The mission is to lead you out of the
shallow breath, into tissue depth.
Away from re-action, toward
contemplative action.
I wish to guide you gently, but sometimes have
to pry off the mask that clings like flesh, break
you free from the prison of your own mind.
Your busy life. Your un-ending drive to conquer
tasks, lists, and the lines on your face.
May I summon the courage to separate you,
for some time, from your postures of defense,
labels and judgements, insecurities and stresses,
your fights and furies, financial entanglements,
your worries, your overindulgent runaway train

mind where you can't run on the tracks fast
enough, pushed and pulled in a multitude of
directions at the same time causing an asterisk
of weariness, neck pain, and sleepless nights.
Please allow me to serve you, purge you from
grabbing, getting, keeping, holding on so tight,
prizes that satisfy the many goals of this life.
May I have the strength to keep you riveted
moment to moment, a breath, a leg, a foot,
the floor, reach, bend, twist your spine,
a new direction for the busy mind.
Look inside, suspended, upended,
wrung out, messy.
I should have, could have, and oh God I didn't.
It's okay.
It's time to give yourself over to
the earth beneath your mat,
return to the cradle, into the heart of
a child before life's traumas and losses,
before responsibilities and obsessions
summoned your attention.
May you rest now like death to honor
the light inside you, still as sunshine.

GODDESS POSE
(UTKATA KONASANA)

To all mothers, sisters, daughters, aunts, female friends, I honor you.

Your struggle to be thin and sexy and beautiful.

May you free the warrior who lives inside your child.

May you always find your footing after birthing and moon cycling.

Step into your power, your purpose, your prowess without shame or guilt or fear.

May you feel the sacredness of who you are with each step on our mother.

You've walked many miles to unveil the purity of your intuition, intellect, and grace.

Know that you're wanted beyond the beauty you strive for, the desire to attract men with.

We need your counsel, your compassion, your vision of peace, your sanctity of love, your earthly wisdom to balance the male ego, war, and pettiness. May you hear your calling whatever it may be and may you act without hesitation.

BREATH

She moves down from above
Warm ocean air
Fills me with her majestic beauty
I hear waves pounding on shore
She waits patiently for him at the door
He rises up from below
Surrenders to her completely
They embrace, merge, dance only for a moment
He receives her unyielding strength
She, his primordial protection
He leaves knowing they will meet again
She waits for him to return over and over

MEDICINE

Extracted from ancient texts.
The Vedas, Sutras, Krishnamacharya,
Yogananda, mantras to the masses.
Extracted from ancient spirit songs
and the voice of knowledge.
The Indigenous American, Chief Seattle, Red
Cloud, Sitting Bull, the blood of their people
soaked in the soil, the land under our feet.
Thousands of years of your prayers are in the air,
I can feel them when I breathe.
The spirits of the executed come through in
rhythmic beats from a drum struck long ago.
Sometimes I feel their suffering when my heart
is close to the earth and pounds in tandem.
Sometimes I hear their call to acknowledge
all relations, creatures, animals.
When my mind is clear and heart is open
after asana, I say Aho Mitakuye Oyasin.

WARRIOR ONE
(VIRABHADRASANA I)

There are some things you must fight for
Every day I fight
Just to maintain my direction home
I fight with indignation, what's right

Sometimes I'm afraid, so I fight
Create bad situations, to fight my way out
I love to fight
It feels good

Without a fight, things accumulate
Thoughts like popcorn on the stove
The fight begins inside, then follows me out
I take my stance and the fight begins

I raise my sword like a shield
It passes through time
Pushes against my chest
Pounds it out, softens my gaze

I fight for the honor of living in a body
I fight for the family of sole survivors
The right side of history in time
A good fight, a whiskey, or a wine

WARRIOR TWO
(VIRABHADRASANA II)

Open with words to hips, chest, arms, stretch.
Heal in death or next steps in breath.
Neither male nor female, angry nor sad.
The warrior emerges in our child when it's safe,
lives beyond the walls of the flesh like faith.
Or it crawls into the caverns of
our joints to play dead.
We must be intimate to authentically connect.
Screen glare, sparkly things, and gadgets
steal our attention away from the natural.
The warrior needs to feel the space in-between,
where boredom fuels our dreams.
The space without the walls of doubt,
unlimited by the condition of our youth.
The warrior is the spirit self, becomes
truth through spirit help.

Practice the warrior, the world
needs your service.
Practice the warrior, buds burst
open when winter is over.

EAGLE POSE
(GARUDASANA)

Perched without fear.
Wrapped like a present.
Like no other winged one
the eagle flies closest to heaven.
The eyes of God come through spirit songs,
messages from creation.
Cultures blend through layers of rock
and winds howl through cracks.
The time to listen
with the eagle's vision
is here now.

HALF MOON POSE
(ARDHA CHANDRASANA)

The moon is not mine,
sand grain rusty nail heads poke through the
flaking porch floor.
Crowbar is bent,
wind doesn't care.
Pull them out with fingertips.
One by one.
The blue-sky heron drifts formally, wings shadow
the pond, flag hangs dead.
A loon calls too far away to sell.
Judge pointed to my prison.
Loud steps.
River rock cracks near sharp corners.
Razor dulled
I love her so.

TREE POSE
(VRKSASANA)

Babies move like water. Silky skin merges with skeleton, the walk begins.
Playing, pushing our limits in single digits.
Our first decade shapes our landscape.
Flexible teenagers carry back packs. Books and baggage, love hurts, wine feels good.
College, work, money. Dreams and credit cards, navigational fortitude. Vocational or practical, work first, art later.
Step into challenge with talent, the payoff is higher.
Practice moving before old age takes you over. Sit still to sit still window sill while birds flutter.
The new generation runs on screen, digital grass stain, forest green.
The distance between you and I is one laugh or one cry, one dusk or one dawn.

Stress makes you stiff. Muscles grab.
Stay in touch with trees, stand among them,
humble and just breathe.

THE PRAYER
(SUKHASANA, ANJALI MUDRA)

I sit on a carpet of needles and
roots amidst towering spruce.
Trunks creak and crack as the wind
howls through their tops.
The scent of pine shines my bones,
rays of sunlight spider through.
I take several deep breaths to
move in past the flesh,
then follow a slow exhalation all
the way into my chambers.
God waits at the table.
Meetings with leaders need the breath.
Watch the breath and talk to
the God living inside.
Faith, not fear, the body is the church.
No body, no temple.

Keep it clean, sturdy, moving, and still.
Move like an animal.
Animals need not pray.
God is never absent.

STRADDLED FORWARD BEND
(PRASARITA PADOTTANASANA)

Feet wide apart, arches lift.
Legs strong.

Hinge at the hips,
release all twenty-four vertebrae.
Let the head be heavy to help.
Oxygen rich blood flushes your brain and face.
The pressure change is worth the time it takes.
Anytime you feel trouble on the
spine or a worried mind.
Whenever you need to freshen up.
Open your step,

hang down,
release your breath, refresh.

HEAD STAND
(SIRSASANA)

Inversions change internal pressure.
Pressure and time create diamonds.
Invert your body,
reverse the flow of interstitial spaces,
electric currents defy gravity.
Pituitary stimulates pineal opportunity.
The world behind the veil, revealed.
Greed gets the best of men who lie to win.
The body never lies.
Stand on the clouds.
Link the mind.
Listen to the sunrise.

CAMEL POSE
(USTRASANA)

Kneeling humbles.
On the pew, every Sunday.
Teenagers denounce religion.

Never sold my soul.
Brother shot himself dead.
On my knees, again.

Crippled
Contracted

unblessed
unfiltered
unwilling
unraveled.

If I die my light will never shine.

I pressed my hips forward.
Arched back.
Opened up.
Screamed out.
Ripped open.
Torn apart.
Fell to pieces.

Finally rested.
Went back to the start.

Became a hummingbird.
Then the flower

Still moments
Move slow
Darkness cracks
Light streams in
Spirits dance
moonlight wind

WHEEL POSE
(URDHVA DHANURASANA)

Tied to the past with domestic braids,
we open channels through the front line.
The distance from joint to joint is short,

lengthen them all at the same time.
Do the wheel over and over.
Push back against the walls of
the world closing in.
Push back on decisions we
want to do over again.
Push back to create space for what's ahead.
Push hope through the
physical turn it into faith.
In any given moment stand in the face of hate.
Yourself or another hate is not safe.

Causes us to contract instead of expand.
Reflection heals projection.
Ground down, spiral in, open up.

DRAGONFLY
(MAKSIKANAGASANA)

I see out with insight
Breathe in the outside
Turn it upside down
Look up for more
Turn it around.

I hear crickets at night
Frogs talk around the lake
I hear tires on the road in the distance
All the way till daybreak.

Corn fields and pathways
Dirt tracks on the driveway
Green all the way through town.

Rays of sun light transform my wings
I am the bear
I am the buffalo
I am the hawk
Without a care.

Run through the woods with me
I am a runner dodging trees.

Break out of the cocoon of lies
Turn my shadow into wings to fly.

I am a butterfly with dragon's breath
I am a dragonfly without a net.

THE BODY

I hear the rally cry, wolves howling
people hear it
Even the squirrels in the city
A tomato from the garden over synthetic packaged
jargon
Chestnuts roll off the sidewalk smashed on the
street
Facial expressions change online
Backyards landscaped with vegetables and fruit
trees reinvent the farmer
Invest in dirt,
good neighbors instead of pesticides
Everything is fake, the people, the food, research.
Who's paying for the proof, the facts, everyone is
a brand selling, but something must be real.
The body.
The earth sings along, but can't ignore the piles
of plastic floating in the sea.

Everything is all over.

Professor Carbonaro in Earth Science said, "everything must go somewhere and when everything is everywhere, humankind has lost their way."

Now I know why he loved his vodka.

We need the right people to help us get back.

Leaders need healers to help lay down the tracks.

The earth doesn't need saving, she'll shake us off at will.

She's been through ice ages, volcanoes, and fires from hell.

The people need saving, renegotiate what's for sale.

The people need saving from the egos urge to prevail.

When winning is more important than sharing, we all lose.

HALF PIGEON POSE
(EKA PADA RAJAKAPOTASANA)

From downward facing dog, I slide my right knee
to my right hand, sit.
How ironic it seems when I enter my hip.
Takes me back into my boyhood.
The tightness delivers me into my grandmother's
house near the woods,
where farmer's fields open into the backcountry
of hardwoods.
I see myself running through the cornfields with
her German Shepherd.
As I bring him to life, I can go deeper.
Another layer, another friend, a little baseball
player, I am again.
Breath comes in the deeper I go, oh dear it hurts,
there's a deer lying in the dirt on the side of the
road as my dad drives by.
I cry, it must have been all alone when it died.

I see colors then open my eyes, I see others.
Press back into downward dog.
Move on to the other side.

SHOULDER STAND
(SARVANGASANA)

My shoulders collect stress like dust.
One day not long ago, shoulder blade burn.
Daily worry, anxiety, tension, digital waves weave their way from the keyboard into my fingers, hands, up my arms, shoulders, neck, jaw, and eyes.
The current flows in until, can't turn my head.
My poor, stiff, sore shoulders, rounded forward.
It's time to get down to the ground, press my shoulder blades down and lift my legs up.
I look up through my feet to a whole new world above.
At first unfamiliar thoughts appear, suddenly I'm five years old again.
As I look up the way a child does, my three-year-old nephew wanders over and looks down at me the way an adult does.

He says, "Why you down dare?"

I say, "I'm resting my shoulders on the grass."

He laughs, crawls on down alongside me, and we watch the world go by, blue sky, clouds changing shape, birds fly across the scape, leaves on the trees wave in the breeze.

LOW BACK MEDICINE
(VIPARITA KARANI)

Lie down on your back next to a wall,
swing your legs up,
place a one inch folded blanket under your hips,
trust this.
Breathe deep then
soften right in.
Stay for five minutes.
Come back again soon.

CORPSE POSE
(SAVASANA)

I lie down like a leaf floats in a shallow stream.
The edges round as it brushes against the bank.
I lie down to play dead; my soul watches.
I lie down in silence, my grandmother's
grandfather clock ticking away on a weekday
afternoon in August.
I lie down if only for a few moments to give up
the fight in the chaotic current of this life.
I lie down in honor of everything that has ever
happened to me, sustained me until now.
I lie down without the stories that play over and
over like a song stuck in my head. Even what
other people have said, I can put to rest.
I lie down as a painter, a sculptor, an author with
a clear canvas, a block of clay, a blank page.
I surrender this vessel like a raindrop into a
mountain stream in May.

MY DOG,
SHIVA

Yoga.

You are.

Energy in motion.

Redirection any moment.

Mindful when it's important.

A body of work with moving parts.

Especially when you can see the angles.

Letter to words, paragraph to chapters, a story.

Dot, line, circle, colors filling spaces merge on pages.

Scribbles form pictures and blessings in the wind arrive on time.

Her presence alone gave people wanting
to belong a healing purpose.

Shiva, the divine, feels human emotion
locked inside, licks tears, and sits.

She waits patiently holding space, listens to
heart beats unravel pain buried deep.

She lets you purge it all out and stays with you
until she knows you are free of doubt.

She steps away,

shakes her body aggressively,

finds a safe place to lie down,

listens for another painful sound.

KARMA

Players want more money.
Surgeons talk you into their cut.
Runners get high by mile five.
The next race is up ahead.
Yogi's pray with OM and Namaste.
Priests and monks sit around and pray.
Uber drivers sit for their shift.
Too much sitting makes one stiff.
The front line contracts.
Eye-burn from blue screens.
Body screams.
It's under attack.
Laws protecting the air lifted.
Industries producing toxins move to China.
Voting at the polls matters little.
The ice is melting faster.
Hurricane seasons begin earlier.
More natural disasters.

It's time to get back to what matters.
Can't you see what's happening?
People are resources beyond donors.
People need medicine not dollars.
Our disease is greed and our richest want more.
Therein lies the problem.
They make the laws of government.
And the rest of us follow.
Sometimes we forget who has
the ultimate power.
It's not the ones who play God with a pen.
It's climate change sending a message.
It's the shaman who prays.
It's the clouds who bring the rains.
It's time we listen.
Karma.

FISH POSE
(MATSYASANA)

Our work is in front of us, down, and foreword.
The body takes shape, does what the mind tells
it.
Year after year, head down, arms forward, pressing
buttons, grasping, reaching, bending, hunching.
Sometime or another the heart was hurt, shoul-
ders wrap around it, shield it, fold down upon it,
like prison walls.
The fluid form of childhood drying, molding
into adult structure, functional blasphemy.
The calcification of soft tissue into new granite
counter tops without religion over time.
Get back to God. Not out there, God lives in
your spine and your mind.
Undo what was done unknowingly, mindfully.
Support your heart another way.

Lie down belly up, squeeze your blades back, place
your arms under you, let your stiffness humble you.
Press your heart against the walls of your chest.
When you trust your structure release your head
to gravity.
Take your work behind you, look up and back.

CIRCLE OF LIFE

From the warm dark womb, we open our eyes to bright lights. Our mother lies us down, we look up, eventually roll around, fuss, learn to crawl, sit up with no help, find our legs and take our first steps. We lift our head, look forward and all around, practice getting up and down, learn to fall, gorge on information through adolescence, a body so resilient. We stand tall in our responsibilities, procreate, family, dance, work, stay up late in middle age, play in the sun and star gaze with our kids, send them out on their own, develop a new relationship with our spouse or someone else, begin sitting with more help, walking with a cane, swallowing soup and watching hurricanes on TV, old news, more news, ground hog day, we see flashes of the life we lived, relatives and strangers move around us. We sit even more and when we get up we fuss and groan as our body creeks and cracks. We fall asleep in chairs and eventually lie down the way our mother first put us down, one day we'll close our eyes and see a bright light and it will all make perfect sense, this circle of life.

THE YOGA WAY

Yoga is not about gaining anything, it's about losing everything.

Only when you have lost everything will you realize your fortune.

When you're stripped naked of your goals, culture, and destiny.

Only when you allow yourself to be fully embraced by that which breathes you,

will you know God's love like a warm ocean wave washing over you.

Only when you let go of the drive to be something, will you know that you are everything.

Only when you learn to listen will you be heard.

When you see everyone, you will be seen.

This is the yoga way.

The material world and spirits dancing in the wind.

The yoga way is one of life and death.

Pain and joy.

Manifestation and deterioration.

It is and you are.

YOGA PRACTICE
(ABHYASA)

Love this body, abuse it no more.
Cry fearlessly, rest often.
When the play of innocence is over
train it, challenge it,
listen to it more each passing year.
An even pulse against your ego walls
wittels them thin, they may even fall.
Naked memories hurt rainbows.
Stand like a rock in your bones.
Direct your attention to each and every breath.
Control them audaciously.
Breathe like a steam engine turns.
Move in form
to freedom
back to form.
Report the thoughts without the
judge no matter how dark,
but light the way for the children.
Let them hear you breathe and see you move
for the pure joy of it.
Intimacy is important.

Stoke the fire of discipline for everyone.
Humans embody from infancy to adolescence,
don't be their friend.
What we grow up with is part of our flesh.
To access transcendence, use the breath.
When the breath ceases and knowledge rests,
invite death in,
the way the sun sets in the west.

MY POSTURES, PRAYERS,
AND POEMS JOURNAL

MY DAILY YOGA PRACTICE

_____

_____

_____

_____

_____

_____

_____

_____

_____

_____

_____

_____

_____

_____

_____

_____

_____

_____

What thoughts, feelings,
voices, or visions surface
during my yoga practice?

_____
_____
_____
_____
_____
_____
_____
_____
_____
_____
_____
_____
_____
_____
_____
_____

THINGS I'M GRATEFUL FOR:

_____

_____

_____

_____

_____

_____

_____

_____

_____

_____

_____

_____

_____

_____

_____

_____

_____

_____

...during restful moments
or stillness?

_____

_____

_____

_____

_____

_____

_____

_____

_____

_____

_____

_____

_____

_____

_____

_____

...while I'm walking in
nature or outdoors?

_____

_____

_____

_____

_____

_____

_____

_____

_____

_____

_____

_____

_____

_____

_____

_____

Made in the USA
San Bernardino, CA
22 February 2020